LEONARD CALVERT AND THE MARYLAND ADVENTURE

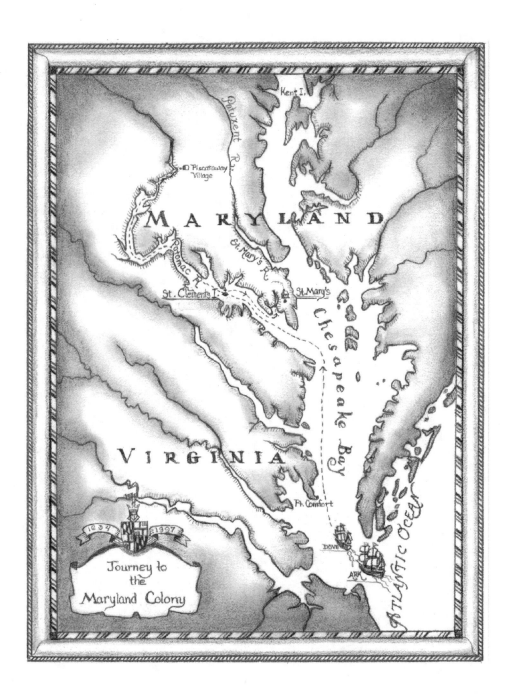

Journey to
the
Maryland Colony

LEONARD CALVERT AND THE MARYLAND ADVENTURE

By Ann Jensen
Illustrations by Marcy Dunn Ramsey

Library of Congress Cataloging-in-Publication Data

Jensen, Ann
    Leonard Calvert and the Maryland adventure / by Ann Jensen ;
illustrations by Marcy Dunn Ramsey. — 1st ed.
        p.   cm.
    Summary: Focuses on the life of Leonard Calvert, the son of first
Lord Baltimore and the younger brother of second Lord Baltimore, the
founder of Maryland.
    ISBN 0-87033-502-2
    1. Calvert, Leonard, 1606?–1647—Juvenile literature.
2. Governors—Maryland—Biography—Juvenile literature.
3. Maryland—History—Colonial period, ca. 1600–1775—Juvenile
literature. [1. Calvert, Leonard, 1606?–1647. 2. Governors.
3. Maryland—History—Colonial period, ca. 1600–1775.] I. Ramsey,
Marcy Dunn, ill. II. Title.
F184.C14J36   1998
975.2′02′092—dc21
[B]   97-39052
                                                                          CIP
                                                                          AC

Manufactured in the United States of America
First edition, 1998; second printing, 2000

To Dr. Lois Green Carr,
Jane McWilliams,
the Maryland State Archives,
and Historic St. Mary's City

A Quiet Boy

Long ago, before Leonard Calvert became the first governor of Maryland, he was a boy in England. He was a quiet boy who liked to take his time before he decided to do something or to speak his mind. At school, other boys called Leonard a dunce and a blockhead.

"Don't listen to them," said Leonard's brother Cecil, who was a year older and wasn't bothered by the things people said. So Leonard didn't.

Some boys, whose grandfathers were knights and barons, thought they were better than Leonard. They said his grandfather, the first Leonard Calvert, was only a country gentleman who raised sheep on his estate in Yorkshire.

"Don't listen to them," said Cecil. And Leonard didn't. He was proud that he shared his grandfather's name. His grandfather was a wise man of few words who was well respected among the people of Yorkshire. Leonard liked visiting his grandfather's country home. He even liked the sheep. In the country, it didn't matter much if he was quiet. He learned how to raise sheep, how to run a farm, and how to hunt. He left the talking to Cecil, who was never at a loss for words.

Cecil was like their father, George Calvert, who was a great talker and a trusted adviser to King James I. The king liked George Calvert because he was honest and loyal and was very useful when the king wanted to get things done. King James made him a knight. From then on everyone called him Sir George.

Leonard was proud of his father.

The king gave Sir George important jobs in the government. He made him his secretary of state, one of the highest offices in the land. He liked the work Sir George was doing so much that the king also made him the Baron of Baltimore. Now, he was a knight and a baron. People could call him either Sir George or Lord Baltimore.

Leonard was doubly proud of his father.

Some day, because Cecil was the first-born son, he would also be called Lord Baltimore. Since Leonard was only the second-born son, he figured that he would always be just plain Leonard Calvert. Maybe he would live in the country and raise sheep. Whatever happened, he decided to let his father and Cecil do the talking.

One thing that Sir George and Cecil hardly ever talked about was religion. The Calverts were Roman Catholics, and for many years, Sir George did not practice his religion. It was not a good time to be a Catholic or to practice any religion other than that of the Church of England. So the Calverts didn't talk about religion. But other people did. Some said that anyone who was not a member of the Church of England should be run out of the country, or thrown in the Tower of London, or beheaded.

"Don't listen to them," said Cecil. Leonard tried not to. And he certainly didn't talk about religion. He didn't want to be beheaded.

When Sir George decided to tell the king and all of England that he was indeed a Catholic, he had to resign as secretary of state. Leonard was sure that soon they'd all be on their way to the Tower of London. But Sir George was still a friend of the king and he had other powerful friends. No one came to take them to prison, and Leonard was much relieved.

From the time that the first settlers landed at Jamestown in 1607, Sir George was interested in the colonies, especially a large North Atlantic island called Newfoundland. Sir George asked the king for a colony there. The king decided that it was a good thing for a loyal friend like Sir George to have a colony, and in 1623 he granted him a charter to a colony in Newfoundland. Sir George called his colony Avalon and sent a group of settlers to begin clearing land and building houses.

Now that Sir George was not a member of the government, he had more time to spend on the settlement of Avalon. In the summer of 1627, Sir George visited his colony and was pleased with what he saw. He hurried back to England and began making plans to return with his family.

Off to Avalon

Sir George lost little time preparing for the move to Avalon. By the spring of 1628, all was ready, and his ship, the *Ark of Avalon*, was waiting at the dock in London. In addition to his family and their servants, Sir George took with him forty other colonists. The Calverts made quite a parade marching up the ship's gangplank.

Leonard, who was now twenty-two, felt very important as he followed his father and his stepmother, the Lady Joan Calvert, onto the ship. Behind Leonard was his fifteen-year-old brother George. Next came Francis, whose age we do not know. Their tutor walked behind them with his cane under his arm and a stern look in his eyes to be sure that George and Francis did not talk loudly or fight and fall off the gangplank.

The boys' sisters Elizabeth and Dorothy, who were nineteen and twenty, urged their brothers to hurry. The girls were anxious to see their cabin and to be sure the servants had not forgotten any of their traveling boxes and chests. Thirteen-year-old Helen was in no hurry. She did not want to leave England and the only home she had ever known. She dragged her feet and had to be prodded by her governess to keep up.

When Leonard reached the deck of the ship, he looked back at the dock. There, Cecil and his wife, the Lady Anne of Arundel, stood waving good-bye. Cecil, who was now twenty-three and just married, was not going adventuring with them to Avalon. Leonard's sisters Ann and Grace also stayed behind.

Leonard stood very tall and straight beside his father as the sailors cast off the lines. Now he was Sir George's oldest son—at least for the month-long voyage to Avalon and for as long as they were in Newfoundland. For a minute, he wished he could change places with Cecil as the *Ark of Avalon* moved away from the dock and down the Thames River. Leonard had never been on a sea voyage. He couldn't imagine what Newfoundland would be like, but he was certain it wasn't like Yorkshire, or any other place he knew in England. He hoped he'd know what to do and how to act and what to say now that he was an adventurer.

During the long days at sea, Leonard listened very carefully when Sir George talked about his plans for the new settlement at Avalon. He paid close attention when his father gave instructions to the other colonists and to his servants about the work they had to do when they reached Newfoundland. Sir George had planned very carefully, but almost from the day of their arrival at Avalon, things went wrong.

First, French privateers appeared off the coast and attacked the English settlers when they went out fishing. The Frenchmen hoped to make Sir George give up his colony and go back to England. Sir George's private soldiers, or men-at-arms as they were called, chased the invaders away, but the Frenchmen came back again and again. While the soldiers were busy chasing the French, the rest of the colonists built their houses and planted their gardens with the seeds they brought from England.

Leonard remembered the things he'd learned about farming on his grandfather's Yorkshire estate and was very helpful. But this definitely wasn't Yorkshire. The seeds they planted so carefully would not grow well in Newfoundland's rocky soil. Then, their goats and cows and other livestock began to die. Nothing seemed to go as Sir George had planned, and the French did not allow them any peace.

"I came to build, set, and sow, and I am fallen to fighting Frenchmen who greatly interfere with the fishing trade," Sir George complained in a letter to his friend the Duke of Buckingham. The Duke did not want Sir George to lose his colony. Since the government of Great Britain and the government of France were not on the best of terms, he asked the king to send two of his warships to help Sir George and his colonists fight the pesky French privateers.

When the king's ships arrived, Sir George ordered the master of the *Ark of Avalon* to prepare to join them in fighting the French. He made Leonard the captain in charge of his men-at-arms, and Leonard worked very hard to get them ready for the upcoming battle at sea. He made sure they had enough guns and ammunition. He counted cannons and cannonballs, muskets, and powder and shot. While Leonard drilled the men-at-arms on the deck of the *Ark*, the ship's master trained his sailors for the upcoming battle at sea. When everyone was ready, the *Ark* and the king's warships sailed out to find the French privateers.

The armed fishing boats of the French were no match for the English fighting ships, which returned victorious to Avalon. As they sailed into port, people lined the shores, cheering and firing their muskets in the air. Sir George gave a party to celebrate the victory, which was the first thing they had to celebrate since they arrived in Newfoundland.

"Huzzah!" shouted the guests when Sir George made a toast to the captains of His Majesty's ships.

"Huzzah!" they cheered after the toast to the master of the *Ark,* and "Huzzah!" everyone cried as Sir George raised his cup to toast Leonard. Leonard decided he liked being an adventurer.

The French would think a long time before they attacked again. Sir George sent Leonard back to England to tell Cecil about all their troubles. George, who had to go back to school, and Helen, who didn't want to be in Newfoundland in the first place, went with him.

In the fall of 1628, the three young Calverts said good-bye to Avalon. They didn't know at the time how lucky they were.

A Sad Face of Winter

Those they left behind spent a terrible winter in Newfoundland. The following summer, Sir George wrote a letter to England's new king, Charles I, the son of James I.

"From the middle of October to the middle of May, there is a sad face of winter upon this land," wrote Sir George. He went on to tell of the bitter cold that froze the land and sea around them. Most of their livestock died, and they couldn't even catch fish. Finally, all they had to eat was salt meat and fish they had stored away in barrels during the summer and fall. Everyone was sick.

"My house has been a hospital all this winter," he wrote, "fifty sick at a time, myself being one; and nine or ten of them died."

Sir George decided that what he needed was a new colony in a warmer climate. He could not face another winter in Avalon. "I am determined to commit this place to fishermen that are able to encounter storms and hard weather," he wrote to the king, "and to remove myself and some forty persons to your Majesty's dominion of Virginia."

Without waiting for an answer, Sir George loaded his ships and sailed for Virginia with the Lady Joan, his remaining son and daughters, and their servants.

The Virginians were not at all happy to see the Calverts arrive. They were afraid Sir George was going to ask King Charles to give him Virginia. Since most of the Virginians were members of the Church of England, they did not like the idea of their colony being ruled by a Catholic. They made life very unpleasant for the Calverts.

Sir George decided he didn't want any part of their colony. So he hurried back to England on the first available ship to ask King Charles for another colony. He left his family to wait for him to return.

When he reached London, Sir George discovered that his enemies in the government were working to keep him from getting a new colony. Some were Puritans who did not like Catholics. They were very powerful in the British Parliament and opposed the Church of England and King Charles. They also opposed any of the king's friends, which gave them another reason to object to Sir George having a colony. He was a friend of the king.

In spite of the Puritans' objections, King Charles gave Sir George a colony north of the Potomac River. There was plenty of land around the great Chesapeake Bay. A bothersome young Virginian named William Claiborne had a fur trading post on Kent Island halfway up the Bay, but no one had laid claim to the rest of the land. Sir George and Cecil were soon hard at work writing the charter for their new colony.

Leonard was happy to know that they were going adventuring again, but that happiness quickly turned to sadness for all of the Calvert family. Four months, six months went by, and there was no sign of the ship bringing Lady Joan, Dorothy, Elizabeth, Francis, and their servants and belongings back from Virginia. As time went on, Leonard and the rest of the family knew that the ship was lost. He never saw his stepmother or his sisters and brother again.

Sir George was very sad, but he could not stop work on his colony's charter. His enemies in England were still trying to prevent him from having a colony. He and Cecil kept their secretaries busy. Because he was now an experienced adventurer, Leonard helped in making plans for the day when the Calverts would set sail for the New World.

At last, the colony's charter was ready for the king to sign. Sir George and Cecil were proud of their work. The charter gave Lord Baltimore almost as many powers as the king—in his colony at least. To show King Charles how grateful he was, Sir George named his colony for the king's Catholic wife, Queen Henrietta Maria. Mapmakers were soon adding the name to their maps of the New World. They wrote "Terra Mariae," which was Latin for Maria's Land. Later, everyone simply called it Maryland, since very few Englishmen knew Latin.

A New Lord Baltimore

Sir George never saw Maryland. On April 15, 1632, two months before the king signed the Maryland Charter, he died. All of a sudden, Cecil was the second Baron of Baltimore, and in a short time, he also was the Absolute Lord and Proprietor of Maryland.

As the new Lord Baltimore, he immediately began planning a voyage to Maryland. The first step was to attract gentlemen adventurers to settle the colony.

Since no one had ever heard of Maryland, Cecil published a paper to tell people about it. Maryland was a place with "air serene and gentle," said the paper, "not so hot as Florida and old Virginia, nor so cold as New England, but between them both having the good of each and the ill of neither."

Before long, seventeen gentlemen adventurers and a few others who could pay for such a trip signed up. But they were not enough to settle a whole colony. More people were needed to cut down trees, build houses, work in the fields planting crops, serve as soldiers, or cook and clean and do other things colonists had to do to make a home in the wilderness. So each gentleman paid the way for several men and a few women who were too poor to pay their own passage to the New World. When they got to Maryland, these men and women, who were called indentured servants, agreed to pay for their passage to the colony with four to seven years of labor. This worked out very well. The gentlemen had help with the hardest work, and when the servants were free from their indenture, they received the right to fifty acres of land, a suit of clothes, a few tools, a barrel of corn, and an opportunity to start a new life, something they could not do in England.

By the summer of 1633, Cecil had a list of about 140 people who were ready to make the long and dangerous trip to America.

At the same time that Cecil was making plans to settle his colony, others in England were making plans to take his colony away from him. They almost made the king change his mind and cancel the charter to the Maryland colony he gave George Calvert. To stop that from happening, Cecil decided to stay in England.

Someone had to lead the adventurers to Maryland though, and with so many enemies about, Cecil could think of only one person to trust. He knew of no one more honest and loyal than his brother Leonard. And besides, he had already been on one colonial adventure.

Leonard was very pleased that Cecil trusted him with such an important job, but he wasn't so sure about being in charge of founding a colony. At least Maryland sounded better than Newfoundland.

"Don't worry," said Cecil. "I know you can do it." And he made his brother Governor of Maryland, and just for good measure, added Lord Chancellor, Chief Magistrate, Chief Justice, and Lieutenant General of the militia as well—which made Leonard worry even more. Most certainly, a person who was a governor, a lord chancellor, a chief magistrate, a chief justice, and a lieutenant general had to make a lot of decisions and do a lot of talking.

Cecil knew that founding a colony was a big job, so he appointed two commissioners, Thomas Cornwallis and Jerome Hawley, to help Leonard. They were older and had invested a lot of money in the Maryland adventure. Cecil was sure they would work hard to help the colony succeed. Cecil also sent along his brother George. With so many enemies, two Calverts were better than one, he figured.

Leonard was beginning to feel better. He persuaded Thomas Greene, one of his boyhood friends, to go along as a gentleman adventurer. And since he was governor, Leonard took with him a secretary and lawyer, Peter Draper, to take care of all the paperwork. He also took personal servants to care for his clothes and prepare his meals and indentured servants to build him a

house and work on his farm and do other things that needed doing when they reached the Maryland wilderness. Maybe being a governor wouldn't be so hard after all.

In September 1633, Leonard kept Peter Draper busy with lists and orders as he began to collect the supplies on a wharf on the River Thames in London. The adventurers had to take enough supplies to last a year, so Peter had a long list. He checked everything as it was loaded onto a pinnace called the *Dove* and another ship named the *Ark,* after the one that carried the Calverts safely to Avalon.

Soon the ships' holds were filled with beads, tools, cloth, and other goods to trade with the Indians; with bags and barrels of food; with barrels of beer, because they couldn't count on safe water to drink; with pots and pans and dishes; with tools and nails for building houses; with shovels, axes, and hoes for farming; with seeds to plant; and even with lumber to build a small boat.

Leonard also made sure the adventurers had guns and powder and shot. They needed such things to protect themselves from pirates prowling the sea and unfriendly Virginians and hostile Indians lying in wait when they reached America. And even if all went well, they needed the guns to hunt for food in the forests of their new home. Leonard remembered how much he'd enjoyed hunting on his grandfather's lands in Yorkshire. From all he'd heard, hunting was very good in the New World.

By the first week in October, almost everyone was aboard the *Ark*. The *Dove*, which was much smaller, carried extra supplies.

When everything was loaded aboard the ships, not much room was left for people. Leonard, his brother George, Thomas Greene, Thomas Cornwallis, Jerome Hawley and his wife, and the other gentlemen adventurers shared cabins. The rest of the men and a few women and boys were crammed into the dark spaces below the ship's main deck.

Once everyone found a spot and settled in as best they could, they waited for the ship to set sail. And they waited. And waited. And waited. Sometimes they paced the deck. Sometimes they walked on the wharf or ventured into nearby city neighborhoods. Days passed and then a week, and the ships were still at the dock in London.

"When will we leave?" the passengers asked Peter Draper, and Peter Draper asked Leonard.

"Soon," said Leonard, who got very tired of answering the same question. He went to his cabin and closed the door to wait like everyone else. And while he waited for Cecil to send word that they could set sail, Leonard worried.

"Don't worry. Your brother knows what to do," said Thomas Cornwallis. But Leonard wasn't so sure.

Cecil's enemies in England were still trying to keep the colonists from leaving for Maryland. The Puritans spread rumors that the Calverts were secretly working for the Catholic government of Spain to take over the English colonies in America. They "defamed the business all they could both publicly and privately, to overthrow it," wrote Cecil.

The adventurers did not leave London until October 19. They sailed down the coast of England to the Isle of Wight, where the English Channel opens into the Atlantic Ocean. There, they made one last stop in the port of Cowes to pick up a few more supplies and final instructions from Cecil.

In mid-November, Cecil's instructions arrived. They were brought by Father Andrew White. Leonard was happy to see Father White, who was an old friend and adviser to the Calverts. He wasn't as happy once he saw the long list of instructions Cecil sent to guide him and Thomas Cornwallis and Jerome Hawley on the voyage and after they reached the New World. He took the list to his cabin and sat down to read.

First, keep the peace among the colonists, Cecil wrote. No fighting and no arguments, especially about religion. Cecil particularly warned the Catholic adventurers against offending the Protestants and giving them reasons to complain to anyone in England or Virginia. Also, treat all men fairly, no matter what their religion, Cecil told Leonard and the commissioners.

Cecil had written many more instructions, which kept Leonard reading and thinking for quite a long time. Look for spies among the passengers and crews of the two ships, Cecil ordered. Find a place to settle. And be sure to choose just the right place. Then, plant corn and build houses, a fort, and a town. Make sure that all of the men receive military training. And, finally, start trading with the Indians and other colonists.

But first of all, the adventurers had to get out of England.

The Maryland Adventure Begins

*U*nfavorable winds and tides kept the ships in the harbor at Cowes until November 22, 1633, when Leonard finally gave the order for Master Lowe to get the *Ark* under way. They signaled the master of the *Dove* and sailed out of Cowes. On November 24, they sailed past the western end of England and were in the North Atlantic. The weather was cold but clear, and the lookouts kept a sharp watch for pirates. The master of the *Dove* sailed the smaller ship close enough to the *Ark* to talk to Master Lowe. He would show two lights from the masthead if he was in trouble, the *Dove*'s master said.

On the first day, Leonard didn't have time to worry. He was too busy stopping fights and not offending the Protestants. He was too busy treating everyone fairly and looking for spies on board the ship and pirates on the sea.

The next day, Leonard forgot about Protestants, spies, and pirates. By evening, lightning split the dark sky, and thunder boomed with the sound of a hundred cannons. Heavy rain and hail beat on the decks, and the ships rolled back and forth in the rough seas. Many of the passengers were seasick. Leonard and his brother George were not. They had been through storms at sea during their Avalon adventure.

Father Andrew White kept a diary and wrote about that first storm. "The winds were all day gathering and toward night poured forth such a sea of wind as if they would have blown our ship under water at every blast," he wrote.

Many of the passengers were not only seasick but also afraid that the ship would break in two. The women cried. The men tried to be brave. Everyone prayed. Most of them had never been on a long sea voyage. Many were leaving England forever, and others didn't know if they'd ever see their families again. All they knew was that ahead of them was a long, dangerous trip and, very probably, more dangers at the end of it.

"Don't worry," Leonard told the other adventurers. "This is a good ship and we have a good master."

"Don't worry," he told his servants and sent them below to comfort the other passengers.

At midnight, the lookout aboard the *Ark* saw two lights in the darkness. The *Dove* was in trouble. The news spread among the passengers. They prayed even harder. Certainly the *Dove* was lost.

The Maryland adventure was off to a very bad start. To lose the *Dove* and her crew was bad enough. But to lose the supplies she carried was even worse. The little ship carried many chests of beads, axes, cloth, and other goods to trade with the Indians. She also carried herb and vegetable seeds to start gardens in the New World, a few pigs, and many of the tools they needed for farming.

Several passengers pleaded with Leonard to turn back. He went to talk to the ship's master.

Master Lowe had spent many years at sea. He had been through many storms. "This is not the worst I have seen," he said.

So Leonard decided. "Sail on," he said.

By morning, the storm had passed and the sea was calm, but nowhere could they see the *Dove*. The passengers crowded belowdecks were cold and fearful, but soon the ringing of the ship's bell reminded them that they were also hungry.

Once a day, with the ringing of the bell at noon, the day's ration of food was handed out. A few passengers and crew members were in charge of preparing the food for the rest. With calm seas, it was safe to build cooking fires in metal braziers on the deck. Everyone welcomed the thought of hot food, even if it wasn't very good, just boiled salt meat, cheese, and hard, dry biscuits. Everyone drank beer, since the water was not safe.

Mealtime was much more pleasant for Leonard and the other gentlemen. They had wine to drink, pickled meats, and spices and other things to make the food taste better. In their cabins, the gentlemen were also much more comfortable. The passengers slept, ate, and spent day after day all together in the same small space with ceilings so low only the shortest people could stand up straight. When the weather was bad and the seas were rough, they were not allowed on deck. They slept on damp, lumpy mattresses, and seldom washed or changed clothes. Many were seasick.

Spirits and Witches

The passengers made the best of a bad situation for the next three days. They thought the worst was behind them, but they were never more wrong.

On the night of November 29, the black clouds appeared like "all the spirits and witches of Maryland were now set in battle array against us," Father White wrote in his journal. A sudden whirlwind tore the mainsail in two and half of it fell into the sea. This new storm was so fierce that even seasoned sailors were frightened. The *Ark* was at the mercy of the winds and waves. She "floated like a dish 'til God was pleased to take pity upon her, " wrote Father White.

Leonard, the other adventurers and passengers, and even Master Lowe and his crew prayed as never before. In his cabin with his brother George, Leonard decided that this was a good time to worry. He didn't expect to see the next day, much less

Maryland. And when the morning did come, the skies were still dark. The storm raged on for another day and night, and then as suddenly as it began, the storm ended.

The next morning brought the first sunshine and calm seas in seven days. The passengers rushed up on deck to breathe the fresh air and dry their damp clothes in the sun. Leonard smiled and nodded as he walked among them. He was very relieved.

Then he caught sight of a lookout high in the crow's nest near the top of a mast and began to worry again. Now that the storm was past, they had to watch out for pirates.

But no pirate ships appeared on the horizon, and the days remained bright and sunny and warm. At first everyone was happy to be warm, but the weather got warmer and warmer, and the passengers were no longer happy. Although it was still winter, every day was "as hot as the hottest day of summer in England," wrote Father White.

Below the main deck, the passengers in their heavy woolen clothes grumbled and complained and got hotter and hotter. In their cabins, Leonard and the other gentlemen were hot too, but they had fresh clothes to wear, fresh air to breathe, and room to stretch and move around. The rest of the passengers wore the same clothes day in and day out. There was never any fresh air and not an extra foot of space to stretch or move in.

Searching for cool breezes, they climbed the ladder to the deck but found none. The winds blew hot across the sunbaked deck, and the passengers grumbled and complained some more. The best they could do was walk around, making sure they didn't get in the way of the sailors sailing the ship. They didn't even have mealtime to look forward to. After more than a month at sea, they were very tired of boiled salt meat. The cheese was moldy, their biscuits were full of bugs, and all they had to quench their thirst was warm beer.

Leonard didn't have to hear the passengers grumbling and complaining. He could see how hot and unhappy they were. He could see their dirty, rumpled clothes and could smell them too. He felt bad, and when Christmas day arrived, he ordered wine for everyone.

Christmas was merry, but afterwards some of the passengers became very sick, perhaps from spoiled food. Richard Edwards, the ship's surgeon, did everything he could. Mistress Ann Cox, one of the women aboard, helped to nurse the sick people. In spite of their efforts, two gentlemen, one of Leonard's servants, and nine other passengers died and were buried at sea.

Leonard was very sad and discouraged. First they'd lost the *Dove* and the people and supplies she carried. Now they'd lost twelve more people. He took out Cecil's long list of instructions, but could find nothing about lost ships and people who died from the heat and bad food. Nor did Cecil write anything about what to do when the passengers grew tired of salt meat, peas, and dry biscuits.

To make matters worse, when he sent someone to check on their supplies, Leonard discovered they were very low on biscuits and other food as well. Even moldy cheese and biscuits with bugs in them were better than nothing at all to eat. A ship full of people with empty stomachs was an unhappy place indeed.

Land Ho!

On January 3, 1634, the lookout's cry of "Land ho!" brought everyone out on deck. A cheer went up when the passengers could make out the distant shore.

"How good it will be to stand on solid ground," said one man.

"I wonder what it will be like?" said another.

"We'll have fresh meat for a change," said a third.

Leonard and his commissioners began making shopping lists of the fresh food and other things to buy when they reached land.

The land, they soon discovered, was the island of Barbados, a British colony in the West Indies. When the *Ark* dropped anchor in the harbor, and Leonard and his commissioners went ashore to buy supplies, they made another discovery. Lord Baltimore's enemies were everywhere.

Perhaps the merchants on Barbados had interests in Virginia, or perhaps they didn't like Catholics. Whatever the reason, they raised their prices so high that only Leonard and George Calvert and the other gentlemen could buy the fresh food they needed for the rest of their trip.

"Nothing could be had but it cost us our eyes," wrote Father White about the high cost of fresh food.

That was a big disappointment to everyone else after living on salt meat for weeks. Leonard and the other gentlemen did send their servants ashore for fresh water and to dig up sweet potatoes that grew wild on the island. "At least the people aboard the *Ark* will have a change from moldy biscuits and warm beer," thought Leonard.

During the twenty days that the Maryland adventurers stayed in Barbados only one good thing happened. Everyone was surprised and pleased one day to see the *Dove* sail into the harbor. She did not sink in the storm, her master told Leonard. Instead, he turned her around and sailed to the nearest port until the storm ended. He then crossed the Atlantic with another ship bound for the West Indies. Leonard was feeling much better when, on January 24, 1634, the *Ark* and the *Dove* left Barbados and headed north.

He felt even better after they stopped at an island along the way and were greeted by two canoes full of friendly Indians. Leonard ordered the captain of the *Dove* to open a chest of the trade goods he had on board and the colonists traded knives, bells, and other things for pumpkins, bananas, and melons. The fresh food made everyone's spirits rise. After several more stops in the West Indies, they reached the American coast and finally sailed into the Chesapeake Bay.

First Stop, Virginia

The two ships arrived at Point Comfort in Virginia on February 27. They had picked up some passengers in the West Indies who wanted to get off there. Leonard also carried letters from King Charles to John Harvey, governor of Virginia. The Marylanders prepared for the worst.

"As for Virginia, we expect little from them but blows," wrote Father White.

Leonard remembered how his father was treated when Sir George and Lady Joan visited Virginia after leaving Avalon. Much to his surprise, Governor Harvey seemed happy to see the Maryland adventurers. He helped them find "all manner of provisions, cattle, hogs, corn, poultry, and fruit trees." He even supplied them with bricks and tiles to use to build a house for Cecil when he came to Maryland. Leonard had to buy another pinnace to carry all the supplies.

Most other Virginians were not happy to see Lord Baltimore's ships drop anchor in the harbor at Point Comfort. One of the unhappiest was William Claiborne. Until Leonard and the other adventurers appeared at Point Comfort, William Claiborne had

had the Chesapeake Bay pretty much to himself. Except for the Indians of course.

Before the first colonists arrived in Virginia and William Claiborne settled on Kent Island, the Indians who lived on the land around the Chesapeake Bay had plenty of room. Sometimes one Indian tribe wandered onto the hunting grounds claimed by another tribe and they fought. The loser then had to look for a new place to hunt, but there was so much land, the Indians believed they always would find someplace to go.

At the same time, in England, people never had enough land. They were crowded together in houses, which were crowded together in villages, towns, and cities. Only the rich, like the Calverts, owned land. For most, good jobs and opportunities for a better life were scarce.

When word got around that anyone who could get to America would find land, and maybe even gold, people like those who sailed with Leonard Calvert decided to leave England. No one asked permission from the Indians, who had lived in America for ten thousand years or more and thought the colonists' New World was a pretty old world and big enough for everyone.

Many Indians made friends with the colonists, who had knives, hatchets, pots, and beads to trade for food and animal furs. The settlers did not find the gold they hoped would make them rich, but the Indians' furs were much in demand in England and were almost as good as gold.

William Claiborne was especially successful at fur trading and making friends with the Indians, even the warlike Susquehannocks. Nearly one hundred people lived around his fur trading post on Kent Island, where the Indians came regularly to trade. There, William Claiborne was in charge and he could do almost anything he wanted. And mainly what he wanted to do was control the fur trade with the Indians. He did not want Kent Island to become a part of Maryland, and he particularly did not want Cecil Calvert, or his brother Leonard, telling him what he could or could not do. He did not want to share the fur trade with them.

While the Maryland adventurers were in Virginia, William Claiborne visited Leonard. "Be careful," he warned. "The Indians are in arms and ready to fight. It is rumored that Spanish invaders are coming to drive them out of the country. They may think you are the Spanish."

"Now who frightened the Indians with tales of Spanish invaders?" Leonard wondered. Who else but William Claiborne, who hoped to make the Maryland adventurers turn back. As Father White wrote in his journal, "The rumor was most like to have begun from himself."

But Leonard said nothing about his suspicions. Cecil had given strict instructions that he was to be courteous to William Claiborne. In fact, Leonard was to tell him that Lord Baltimore would show him "all the love and favor" that he could, if Claiborne cooperated and became a citizen of Maryland. If

Claiborne would not cooperate, Cecil told Leonard, he was to leave him alone for a year, but watch him very closely until the Maryland colony was established. Then Cecil would let Leonard know what to do about William Claiborne. So Leonard listened courteously to William Claiborne's warning and went on with his plans.

Maryland at Last!

The Marylanders stayed in Virginia nine days. They left Point Comfort on March 3, 1634, and sailed up the Chesapeake Bay.

"You will scarcely find a more beautiful body of water," wrote Father White. Leonard and the other adventurers agreed.

Two days later, the three ships arrived at the mouth of the Potomac River, which was the widest, deepest river Leonard had ever seen. The shores were lined with forests of huge trees, "not choked up with under shrubs, but so far distant from each other that a coach and four horses may pass between them without hindrance."

"We found, as we were told, all of the Indians in arms," wrote Father White. The shores of the river were lined with Indian bowmen.

"They made a general alarm, as if they intended to summon all the Indians of America against us," Leonard wrote in a letter back to England. He was more certain than ever that William

Claiborne or some other enemy told the Indians that the Marylanders were coming to their country to destroy them.

The Piscataway Indians, who watched curiously from the shore, had never seen a ship as large as the *Ark*. They had seen only the smaller boats and pinnaces used by William Claiborne and other fur traders and explorers on the Bay. Indians in one village carried word to those in the next that coming up the river was a canoe as large as an island carrying as many men as there were trees in the forest. Indian canoes were made from a single large log, and they could not imagine where the tree grew that could be made into a canoe as large as the one that was carrying the strangers up the Bay.

The Indians followed on land as the *Ark* and the two pinnaces sailed slowly up the Potomac River. Finally on March 5, 1634, the three ships arrived at a small island occupied only by large flocks of herons.

"This is where we will land," said Leonard, and 123 days after the adventurers left Cowes, England, they set foot on Lord Baltimore's province of Maryland. They named the island St. Clement's.

St. Clement's Island was not large enough for a settlement, however. Leonard had to find a place on the mainland, but as they saw on their trip up the Potomac, hundreds of Indian warriors were probably waiting on the mainland with arrows strung in their bows. Leonard first had to make peace with the Piscataway.

Maryland's Founding

Leonard set out to visit the emperor, or tayak, of the Piscataway Indian tribes to let him know that the colonists meant no harm. He left the *Ark* behind at St. Clement's Island. Instead, he took the *Dove* and the other pinnace. They were much smaller and better for exploring because they could sail in shallow creeks and rivers without running aground. With him he took gifts for the Indian emperor and things to trade.

He also took Captain Henry Fleete, a fur trader who joined the Maryland adventurers in Virginia. The captain once lived with the Indians and was "excellent in language, love, and experience with the Indians," wrote Father White. Henry Fleete was a great help in finding the Piscataway emperor.

With Captain Fleete as their guide, the Marylanders sailed up the river to a village the Indians called Potomac. Leonard went ashore with Henry Fleete, Father John Altham, and several others.

Leonard walked at the front of the procession, which was the sort of thing he was sure that governors were expected to do. It was also a wise thing to do, if he wanted to make friends with the Indians. At that moment, Leonard wished that Cecil were there leading the way into the Indian village. When he was not viewing them from the safety of a ship, the Indians looked very fierce indeed. The Indian men were much bigger than any of the settlers, and their faces were painted dark red—"to keep away the gnats," wrote Father White—and "blue from the nose downward and red upward and sometimes, contrariwise with great variety."

Of course, the Englishmen with their beards and mustaches, their guns, and their heavy clothes all belted, buckled, and buttoned looked just as strange and fierce to the Indians. Women peered suspiciously from the shadows inside their houses, and children peeked out from behind trees and bushes. The men stood waiting solemnly as the adventurers came near.

Henry Fleete spoke to the Indians in their own language. He learned that this was not the village of the tayak. The Indian who greeted them was not even a werowance, as village chiefs were called. His name was Archihu, and he was the uncle of the werowance, who was still a child. With Henry Fleete acting as an interpreter, Leonard and Father Altham talked with Archihu and explained that they came as friends. Archihu, who was a grave and considerate man, welcomed them and invited them to return.

His men would hunt and fish for the Englishmen, he said, and they would share whatever they got.

Leonard thanked Archihu and said good-bye. He felt much more confident about meeting Indians when he and his men set sail again. As the *Dove* dropped anchor in the river near Piscataway, however, Leonard's confidence almost left him. Ashore five hundred Indians armed with bows and arrows waited. In front of them, Leonard could not mistake the tayak. He stood tall and straight, his face painted red and blue in a ghastly way. He wore long bird feathers in his black hair. Bear claws, eagle talons, and shells hung around his neck. Animal skins clothed his body.

From the deck of the pinnace, Leonard made signs of peace. He was very relieved when Henry Fleete agreed to go ashore to talk to the tayak. Soon Captain Fleete was back with the Indian emperor and two of his warriors. Leonard invited them into the master's cabin where he had iron kettles, knives, glass beads, and cloth laid out as gifts.

Again Henry Fleete was the interpreter as Leonard asked the tayak's permission to establish a settlement.

"I cannot bid you go, nor can I bid you stay," said the tayak in his Algonquian language, which Captain Fleete translated for Leonard. "Settle wherever you wish."

Leonard returned to St. Clement's Island much encouraged. There he discovered that the men and servants left behind had put together the small boat they'd brought from England and were starting the log fort as he ordered before leaving to visit the tayak.

Soon after their return, Father White's servants made a large cross from trees on the island. Then on March 25, 1634, with Leonard leading the way, the Roman Catholic gentlemen carried the cross to a pleasant spot on St. Clement's Island and put it in the ground. Father White celebrated mass and, on behalf of Lord Baltimore, took possession of the country, "for our Savior and for our Sovereign Lord King of England."

Leonard stood proudly through the ceremony and for the first time since Cecil named him Lord Chancellor, Chief Magistrate,

Chief Justice, and Lieutenant General of the militia, he felt like the governor of Maryland.

Following the ceremony, a group of women servants gathered some clothing and church linen to carry ashore to wash. As they were being rowed in, their boat overturned, and there was great excitement until they were rescued. "The linen they went to wash was much of it lost, which is no small matter in these parts," wrote Father White. They had to wait months for more clothes and linen to come by ship from England.

Finding the Perfect Spot

"I still haven't found what I most wished for, to wit some field cleared and left by the Indians, where we can make our first settlement," Leonard told Henry Fleete.

"Come with me," said Henry Fleete, and Leonard, Thomas Cornwallis, Jerome Hawley, and several of Leonard's servants went with him aboard the new boat. Not far from the mouth of the Potomac, Captain Fleete guided them into another broad and deep river. There, about five miles from the river's mouth, they came to a bay and on high ground above it, large cleared fields.

"This is just what I'm looking for," said Leonard. But there was one problem. The land was occupied by an Indian village. He could see a small group of Indians watching from the bluff above the river.

"Let's go and talk to them," said Captain Fleete, and Leonard gave the order to go ashore. After his experience with Archihu and the tayak, Leonard was not as uneasy when he climbed the narrow trail to where the Indians waited.

"These are Yaocomacos," said Henry Fleete as they walked up to the group at the top of the hill. He did not have to tell Leonard which Indian was the werowance. He was as tall and fierce looking as the tayak, but wore fewer feathers in his hair and fewer bird and animal claws strung on his necklaces.

The werowance greeted the Englishmen in friendship and led Leonard and his party into the village. They stopped outside his house, which was the largest, and he invited them in. Like the other houses of the village, the werowance's was made of bent saplings tied together and covered with grass mats. Its doorway was covered with deer hides sewn together. There were no windows. Inside, Leonard found a large room with a hard-packed dirt floor. Around the sides of the room were platforms covered with animal skins. Leonard and Henry Fleete sat with the chief and his advisers. Indian women brought them wooden platters heaped with fresh roasted deer meat, fish, and corn cakes that had been baked on hot stones.

When they finished eating, Leonard explained why he had come. He ordered his servants to lay out the axes, hatchets, and cloth he brought as gifts for the werowance and his advisers. Leonard fully expected to do a lot of talking before the Indians gave up their village. To his surprise, Henry Fleete told him the werowance was quite ready to leave his village to the colonists. First, he said, they would sleep and then the chief would show Leonard more of the village.

That night, the werowance gave Leonard his own house and his own bed to sleep on. The Indians were taller than most Englishmen, and Leonard found the werowance's bed much roomier than what he was used to. Piled high with animal skins, it was as soft and comfortable as any bed he slept in at home in England. In the darkness, he lay awake watching the glowing embers of the fire in the center of the room and the smoke curling upward through a hole in the roof that arched overhead. The room was smokey and warm. Very warm. Which was fine if you were an Indian and wore only a few loosely fitting animal skins. Even though the night was chilly, Leonard squirmed in his heavy clothes of linen and wool.

Leonard did not go to sleep for a long time. His day had been quite an adventure. He thought about Archihu, the tayak, and the werowance of the Yaocomaco. He tried to remember all of the plans his father made on the voyage to Avalon. But Maryland was very different from Newfoundland. And Sir George made all the important decisions about settling that northern colony. Leonard spent the night thinking of all the decisions he had to make in the coming days.

"Don't worry," he told himself, and finally went to sleep.

He felt much better when morning came and he was outside again doing useful things. The decision making actually was easier than he had thought. Peter Draper, his secretary, hurried close behind Leonard with his pen and ledger book ready to write down Leonard's instructions.

Leonard was very pleased with what he saw as he looked around the village. It sat high above the river, which gave the colonists a safe harbor for ships of all sizes. The steep river banks helped protect the settlement from attack by water.

Captain Fleete "brought us to as noble a seat as could be wished and as good ground as I suppose is in all Europe," Father White wrote. "Is it not miraculous that a nation that was in arms against us and our enterprise a few days before should like lambs yield themselves, glad of our company, giving us houses, land, and livings for a trifle?"

Actually, it was no miracle that the Indians gave up their land so easily. Even before the English colonists arrived, the Yaocomaco were planning to abandon their village and move across the Potomac River to Virginia. They were peaceful farmers and hunters who lived in fear of the warlike Susquehannocks who came down from the north to raid their village. Many had already left.

Now, in addition to the river, the Yaocomacos had an English settlement between them and Susquehannock raiding parties. The Indians agreed that colonists could live in one part of their town and they would live in the other so that they could tend their corn fields. When they harvested the corn, the werowance promised, the Indians would share it with the colonists and then leave the rest of the village and their corn fields to the English.

When Leonard looked toward the outskirts of the village, he could see the Indians already preparing the ground to plant corn. They were chopping at the rich, black earth with hoes made of sticks and the flat shoulder-blade bones of deer.

"Be sure we have plenty of hoes to trade with the Indians," Leonard told Peter. He guessed that the Indians' tools took a long time to make. English tools of metal would save them time and most certainly would last longer than bones.

Beyond their fields, Leonard saw forests where the settlers could find more than enough wood to build their houses.

"Everyone must begin planting and building houses," ordered Leonard, and Peter wrote it down. "Until our houses are built, we will live in those the Indians have left," Leonard added. He also chose one Indian house to be used as a storehouse for supplies from the ships, one for a guardhouse, and one for a chapel. He sent the boat back to St. Clement's Island with orders for the other settlers to join them.

To Make a Town

At first, most of the colonists slept on the *Ark* at night and spent their days unloading supplies and moving into the Indians' houses.

When they were all moved into the village, Leonard ordered a grand celebration. The werowance of the Patuxents, whose tribe lived nearby, joined the werowance of the Yaocomacos to watch the English ceremony.

Leading the other gentlemen adventurers from the *Ark*, Leonard went ashore where his guests were waiting. His men-at-arms carried the English flag and one for the Barony of Baltimore and everyone marched to the village. When they arrived they fired their guns in a salute. The Indians, who realized they had to get used to these strangers and their noisy weapons, stood solemnly as the cannons on the *Ark* thundered an answer.

Leonard made a short speech and announced that the new settlement was named St. Mary's in honor of the Virgin Mary. The Indians brought food—hominy and corn cakes, oysters roasted in their shells, smoked deer meat—and the celebration ended with a feast.

There was so much to do to turn the village in the wilderness into a town that Leonard didn't have time to worry about making decisions and giving orders. He just did it. He kept Peter Draper busy making lists and sending messages. Leonard sent a boat to Virginia with an order for fourteen cows, thirty pigs, and a flock of chickens. He and Thomas Cornwallis made plans for a fort and put their carpenters and other servants to work building it.

When the fort was finished, Leonard wrote to a friend in England. "We have seated ourselves within one-half mile of the river, within a palisade of 120 yards square with four flanks. We have mounted one cannon and placed six smaller guns in parts most convenient, a fortification, we think, sufficient to defend against any such weak enemies as we have reason to expect here."

The adventurers were getting tired of living in the Indian houses, and when they finished the fort, they sent their servants into the nearby forests for more timber to build English-style homes. They also got to work planting the vegetable seeds and

the fruit tree seedlings they had brought from England. Thanks to the Indians, they had cleared fields and garden plots.

"We'll have no starving time in Maryland," Leonard thought. He remembered the stories he'd heard about the early years of the Virginia colony when winters without food cost many lives, and he was very grateful to the Yaocomacos.

But it was hard to think of winter during springtime in Maryland. How different it was from Avalon with its rocky soil.

"The soil is so excellent, we cannot set down a foot but tread on strawberries, raspberries, fallen mulberry vines, acorns, walnuts, sassafras, and the like in the wildest woods," wrote Father White. "All is high woods except where the Indians have cleared for corn. It abounds with delicate springs, which are our best drink. Birds diversely feathered there are infinite, as eagles, swans, herons, geese, ducks, partridge, red, blue, parti-colored."

New Friends

The friendly Yaocomaco and Patuxents helped the colonists with planting corn and also taught them how to plant other native crops, such as pumpkins and other squash and sunflowers. Yaocomaco women taught the English women how to prepare corn pone and hominy and how to cook other vegetables that were new to the colonists.

The colonists were impressed by the skills of the Yaocomaco hunters, who went into the forests armed only with bows and arrows. "I have seen them kill at twenty yards distance, little birds of the bigness of sparrows," wrote Father White. The Indians, he wrote, "daily catch partridge, deer, turkeys, squirrels, and the like of which there is wonderful plenty, but as yet, we dare not venture ourselves in the woods to seek them, nor have we leisure."

Most of the colonists had lived their whole lives in towns or villages in England. Unlike Leonard, they didn't know how to hunt. What if they met a fierce bear, a mountain lion, or wolf in the forest? Better to leave the hunting to the Indians. Also, they were too busy to hunt, what with all the planting and building they had to do.

Besides, the Indians were eager to trade their fish, game, furs, and corn for clay pipes, iron knives, fishhooks, axes, hoes, sheets of copper, linen shirts, combs, fabric, and other English items. They came to St. Mary's with bear and beaver furs, with deer and other meat, with huge turkeys weighing as much as fifty pounds, with fish of all kinds, and with baskets full of oysters as large as horses' hooves. They also brought corn to trade.

When the *Ark* went back to England in the late spring of 1634, Leonard sent a big order for more cloth, glass beads, combs, brass kettles, axes, knives, hoes, and other metal tools for trading with the Indians, as well as manufactured goods and other supplies the colonists needed. He also sent Cecil two Indian arrowheads, which were a part of what was owed to the king for the Maryland Charter. Every year at Easter time, Cecil was supposed to present the king with two arrowheads. He was also supposed to give the king one-fifth of any gold and silver found in Maryland. Leonard never found any gold or silver, but the Indians were happy to supply him with arrowheads for the king.

Every so often, Leonard sent Cecil a gift. Once, he sent a live deer and would have sent a mountain lion, but it died. Another time, he had a red bird "and kept it a good while to have sent it to you," he wrote his brother, "but I had the ill fortune to lose it by the negligence of my servant who carelessly let it out of the cage."

One of the most important things he sent back to Cecil was a copy of Father Andrew White's diary of the trip to Maryland. When Cecil read Father White's diary, he was so pleased that he had it published as a pamphlet, entitled *A Relation of the Successful Beginnings of the Lord Baltimore's Plantation in Maryland*. In the pamphlet, Cecil invited other adventurers to settle in his colony. Ships soon began arriving with more settlers.

That first spring and summer in Maryland, the colonists' gardens were full of beans, peas, squash, pumpkins, and other vegetables. The corn grew tall in the fields.

"We will not starve next winter," thought Leonard. But that was not what worried him most. Just as in Avalon, soon after the colonists arrived they came down with typhoid fever, malaria, dysentery, the flu, and other diseases. Almost everyone got sick during their first year in America. They called that first year of sickness their seasoning. In St. Mary's, as the weather grew warm and then hot, Leonard's brother George and many other settlers became very ill. The ship's surgeon, Richard Edwards, who wasn't feeling too well himself, was a busy man. He knew about mending broken bones and pulling teeth, but he did not know much about the real causes of diseases and he did not always know the best way to treat them. Too many of the adventurers and their servants died. George was one of those who died.

Leonard sent a letter with the sad news back to Cecil and the rest of the family on the next ship to England. But he could not grieve for long. The same ship that took his letter brought more settlers and more orders from Cecil.

Not Yet a City

You must build a town," wrote Cecil, who imagined that one day St. Mary's would be a place where houses and shops lined the streets like in an English town. He imagined busy markets where farmers brought their vegetables and fruits and their cattle, hogs, and chickens to sell. Inns and taverns would be full of people who came to town to take care of legal matters in court, pay their taxes, and do other government business.

One of the first houses built was for Leonard, and for Cecil, when he finally got to Maryland. It was a one-story, wood-framed house, fifty feet long and eighteen feet wide, and had a parlor and hall with huge fireplaces. Because he was the governor and his house was the largest, with plenty of room for meetings and other gatherings, it was used for government business. It sat in the center of what Leonard hoped one day would be a town.

St. Mary's had very few other public buildings, just the barest necessities. Scattered here and there along the dirt paths that served as streets were a storehouse, Thomas Cornwallis's mill, the Catholic chapel, a cooper's shop, a sawyer's yard, and a blacksmith's forge to repair broken tools and wagon wheels.

Most of the other buildings were Indian houses and small rough-sawn clapboard cottages. They were very simple houses, but they put roofs over everyone's head to keep out the rain. At least most of the time they did.

Although the settlers found plenty of clay for making bricks, which, as Father White wrote, were "as good bricks as any in England," they used them only for foundations and storage cellars. Instead of bricks, many chimneys were made of wood and clay, or wattle and daub, as the colonists called it. Brick houses had to come later. With so many people sick and dying and so much work to do, no one had time or hands to build large brick houses like they had in England. Leonard was certain that Cecil would be disappointed in the capital city of his province, but what could they do?

Thomas Cornwallis tried to help and wrote a letter to Cecil describing his house. "I am building a house to put my head in of sawn timber framed, a story and half high with a cellar and chimneys of brick to encourage others to follow my example, for hitherto we live in cottages, and for my part, I have not yet had leisure to attend my private convenience nor profit, which is not a little necessary for me, having run myself and fortune almost out of breath in pursuit of the public good."

Jerome Hawley also had a comfortable house, and his wife, Eleanor, took care of directing the servants and seeing that everything ran smoothly. Thomas Greene and Thomas Cornwallis left their wives at home in England. Leonard had no wife. They had stewards, but that wasn't the same as having a wife to take charge of running a house, which was a big job. There were very few women among the early settlers and most of those were indentured servants. They couldn't marry until their indenture ended.

Leonard, Thomas Greene, and Thomas Cornwallis looked forward to an invitation to dinner with the Hawleys and dressed with special care. They sat down at a table set with glazed earthenware, silver, and fine glassware. Under the watchful eye of Mistress Hawley, the servants always put before them a proper meal of pork, chicken, turkey, goose, fresh-baked cornbread, milk, cheese, and butter. In late spring, summer, and early fall, the guests also had fresh vegetables, salads, and fruits. When Thomas Greene's wife arrived in 1638, Leonard was a frequent dinner guest at his friend's home as well.

Lawmakers and Lawbreakers

By the end of the first year, Leonard and his commissioners decided that they needed some laws to help them govern the new colony. The Maryland Charter said that an assembly of freemen was to meet to vote on and propose the laws for the colony—with Cecil's approval, of course. So, in February 1635, Leonard sent messages to all of the plantations for the freemen—that is, all white men who were sixteen or older and not servants—to come to St. Mary's for the first General Assembly. Only a few colonists attended the meeting. They gathered at Leonard's house. He didn't have enough chairs, so everyone, except himself, Thomas Cornwallis, Jerome Hawley, and the secretary, stood during the meeting.

The assemblymen were eager to talk, and each one had his own ideas for new laws. But would they ever agree? Leonard wondered. There was much moving around and talking out of turn, and Leonard, who was in charge, spent a lot of time banging on the table and calling for quiet. People outside could hear the noise.

That day, several Indians were in St. Mary's to trade. They peeked in the windows of Leonard's house to see what all the commotion was about and left shaking their heads. How did they ever get anything done with everyone speaking at once? When the Indians had meetings, everyone waited for his turn to speak and decisions were made in a calm and orderly manner.

Leonard also was wondering if anything would ever get done. To his surprise, when the meeting finally ended several days later, he had a long list of new laws. The secretary neatly wrote out a copy of the list and Leonard sent it off to Cecil on the next ship for England. As fast as a ship could bring his answer, Cecil replied. He was not pleased.

"I will suggest the laws for my colony," said Cecil, who felt Leonard and the other colonists needed to be reminded to whom Maryland belonged. "Next year, I will send you a draft of the laws I propose, and you may call another assembly to approve them."

Leonard was glad he didn't have to call the assembly right away. The freemen would not be happy with Cecil's answer. Leonard had a more pressing problem to deal with, anyway.

In the year since their arrival in Maryland, Leonard had left William Claiborne alone. As Cecil instructed, he wrote their old enemy a letter, telling William Claiborne that Lord Baltimore did not intend "to do him any wrong."

The fur trader would have none of it. As far as he was concerned, Kent Island and his trading post were a part of Virginia, not Maryland. Since the Marylanders arrived on the Chesapeake, the Indians were less friendly than they used to be, and he had fewer and fewer beaver skins to ship to England. His customers were beginning to complain.

William Claiborne was determined to show Lord Baltimore that neither he nor his brother Leonard could tell him what to do. He regularly ignored Cecil's order against trading with the Indians. In the spring of 1635, he even went so far as to send Captain Thomas Smith with the pinnace *Long Taile* to trade with the Indians near St. Mary's.

That was too much. Leonard sent Captain Henry Fleete to stop the trading. When he found the *Long Taile,* Captain Fleete seized the boat. Captain Smith was ordered to sail the *Long Taile* to St. Mary's. When William Claiborne learned what happened, he was so angry that he sent armed men aboard the sloop *Cockatrice* to recapture the *Long Taile.* They were ready for a fight when they met two Maryland pinnaces, the *St. Margaret* and the *St. Helen,* in Pocomoke Sound, but it was their unlucky day. Thomas Cornwallis, an experienced soldier, was captain of the *St. Margaret.* In the fierce battle that followed, one Marylander

was killed, but three of the Kent Islanders were lost and three wounded before they fled. William Claiborne was not at all happy that his men were defeated once more by the Marylanders.

What he didn't know was that his troubles had only begun, and all because of the Calverts.

Neither a Dunce nor a Blockhead

William Claiborne's partners in England wanted more beaver skins—many more. He wrote and explained that unfriendly Indians attacked his people on Kent Island, and the Marylanders greatly hindered his trade. His partners weren't interested in excuses. In 1636, they sent George Evelyn to take over the fur trading post on Kent Island and ordered William Claiborne back to England to explain what was going on.

At first this did not look good for Maryland, or for Leonard. George Evelyn was no friend of the Calverts. He wrote about Leonard to a friend in England. "What was his grandfather but a grazier? What was Leonard himself at school but a dunce and a blockhead, and now has it come to this, that such a fellow should be governor of a province and assume such lordly airs?"

Shortly after his arrival, George Evelyn went to see Leonard. He was quite prepared to take up William Claiborne's fight with the Marylanders and put Leonard Calvert in his place. When they met face-to-face, however, George discovered that although Leonard was still on the quiet side, he definitely was not a dunce or a blockhead. And when Leonard did speak, he knew what he was talking about. He also appeared honest and fair, and although he was the governor of Maryland, Leonard spoke plainly and didn't put on lordly airs. So Leonard talked and George listened, and the more George listened, the more he agreed that Kent Island rightfully belonged to Lord Baltimore. Together, they decided what to do about the Kent Islanders.

The residents of Kent Island were still loyal to William Claiborne. They didn't like George Evelyn any more than they liked the Calverts. To make matters worse, the leader of the Kent Islanders was Captain Thomas Smith, who was still angry over losing the battle to the Marylanders in Pocomoke Sound. He refused to accept George Evelyn as the new commander of Kent Island or to submit to the laws of Maryland and Lord Baltimore.

Leonard finally decided to take matters into his own hands. He, George Evelyn, and Thomas Cornwallis gathered about thirty "choice musketeers" led by militia sergeant Robert Vaughn and set off up the Bay. They were prepared for a great battle when they went ashore on Kent Island just before sunrise one morning in February 1638.

Cautiously, they crept up to the fort, expecting at any minute to be discovered. But they weren't. All was quiet. The main gate of Kent Fort was barred, but one of the musketeers found another entrance that had neither bars nor guards. One by one, the Marylanders slipped into the fort. Not a guard, not a soul in sight. Had the Kent Islanders fled? Was it a trap? Inside the barracks, they got their answer. Everyone was sound asleep. By the time the sun was up, Leonard and his men had captured the Kent Islanders without firing a single shot.

Leonard stayed on Kent Island to help George Evelyn establish law and order. He offered to forgive anyone willing to accept Lord Baltimore as the authority in Maryland. One hundred and twenty men came forward. Thomas Smith was not one of them. Leonard had him taken prisoner and sent him to St. Mary's. There he was tried for piracy and hanged. At first Leonard ordered Smith's property seized, which was the sort of thing a governor did with the property of pirates and other criminals. Then he learned that Thomas Smith left a widow and two young daughters. How could he take their home? The more Leonard thought about it, the more he realized that he couldn't. Besides, he was the governor and the lord proprietor's brother. He could be kind and humane and change his mind. If he could order the property seized, he could order it given back, and that was what he did. Leonard returned the family's home to them, and he felt much better.

Having done all he could do on Kent Island, Leonard returned to St. Mary's. George Evelyn also went back with him. He decided he did not want to live on Kent Island and took land near St. Mary's instead.

Law and Order

Not long after George Evelyn arrived in Maryland, another ship dropped anchor in the harbor off St. Mary's. This one brought John Lewger, appointed by Cecil to be Maryland's secretary of state. "Secretary Lewger," thought Cecil, "will be a big help to Leonard with the business of running the colony."

Leonard and Thomas Cornwallis, who often disagreed, were of one mind where Secretary Lewger was concerned. They did not like him very much. Thomas let Cecil know how he felt the next time he wrote. Secretary Lewger, he said, was "not so perfect as I could wish him." He was "too stiff a maintainer of his own opinions," Thomas went on to say, and was "too forward in suggesting new businesses for his own employment." In other words, he didn't listen to what other people had to say and was too bossy and self-serving.

The fact that the secretary brought a long list of laws that Cecil wanted passed at the next meeting of the General Assembly did not make Leonard any happier to see him. The colonists had been in Maryland almost four years and had strong ideas about how they wanted to be governed. They weren't going to be pleased to learn that Cecil rejected the laws they passed at the last meeting.

Leonard was nervous as the assemblymen arrived early on the morning of January 25, 1638. Since the first meeting, they had made rules for how they were to behave. The Indians would have been pleased to see the change. Anyone who got up to speak had to take off his hat. If two or three or more freemen wanted to say something, Leonard had to decide which one spoke first.

That first morning, Leonard had a lot of deciding to do. Almost everyone had something to say about Cecil's list of laws. When all of the talking was done, the assemblymen voted not to accept them. Instead, they chose a committee, including Leonard, Thomas Cornwallis, and George Evelyn, to make a list of the laws they wanted.

"The body of laws you sent over by Mr. Lewger I endeavored to have passed by the assembly, but could not effect it," Leonard wrote to Cecil when he sent the committee's list. "There were so many things unsuitable to the people's good. Others have been passed and now sent unto you, which I am persuaded will appear unto you to provide both for your honor and profit as much as those you sent us did."

Some of the colonists' laws were very good, Leonard thought. It was a crime, for instance, to assault and beat the governor or cut out a person's tongue—he liked those particularly. Anyone accused of these crimes, said the law, "shall suffer the pains of death by hanging except if the offender can read…then, the offender shall lose his hand or be burned in the hand or forehead with a hot iron and shall forfeit all his lands." Reading was a valuable skill, not to be wasted.

Leonard was very relieved when a letter from Cecil arrived to say that he accepted the laws the General Assembly proposed.

Like his father before him, Cecil was a wise man. He had enough enemies in England and Virginia. He did not have to fight with his own colonists. If the Assembly wants to make its own laws, he wrote to Leonard, let them make "such laws as you shall think fit and necessary for the good government of Maryland." Of course, Cecil could still refuse to accept any law he didn't like.

More and more people were arriving in Maryland. Most were indentured servants who were immediately put to work by their masters. As soon as a freeman came ashore, he wanted the land that Cecil promised. Keeping track of who settled where was a big job, and Leonard already had more work than he could handle. As he wrote to Cecil, "The public services of the colony and the necessary looking after some means of my own subsistence requireth much time and labor."

Grudgingly, Leonard had to admit that John Lewger was a big help. The secretary was in charge of distributing land, which caused Leonard to think more kindly of him. He noted in a letter to Cecil that John Lewger was "a very serviceable and diligent man and a very faithful and able assistant to me."

Old Friends

Being a governor was a big job. It was a lonely job sometimes, too. Since his brother George died, Leonard had few real friends who liked him just because he was Leonard Calvert.

Thomas Greene was a true friend, but most others wanted to be his friend because he was the governor and Lord Baltimore's brother.

All that changed in November 1638. That month, a ship from England brought Margaret and Mary Brent and their brothers Giles and Fulk. The Brents and the Calverts were long-time friends. Now Leonard wasn't so lonely. The Brents were a wealthy family. They built not one but two houses, one for Margaret and Mary and one for Giles and Fulk. As soon as Margaret and Mary's house was built, Leonard was there for dinner. He was a frequent guest.

In a short time, the Brents were very important people in Maryland government and business. It did not hurt that they were friends of the Calverts, but they were also very good at buying, selling, and lending.

In addition to land in St. Mary's, Cecil gave Giles all of William Claiborne's land and property on Kent Island. There, Giles built a large house and mill and kept a herd of one hundred cows. In Virginia, where he was living, William Claiborne vowed to take revenge one day on the Calverts and especially their friend, Giles Brent.

Margaret Brent became an important and successful businesswoman. When new settlers needed money, she loaned it to them. When they didn't pay her back, she took them to court and acted as her own lawyer. She was very good at that, and soon other people were asking her to handle their cases in court.

Leonard always knew that he could go to Margaret for advice. And he often did.

The Brents joined Leonard in 1640 for a very special wedding. According to Indian custom, a man could have several wives. When Kittamaquund, the tayak of the Piscataway, decided to become a Christian, he chose just one wife and they were baptized and married in a Christian ceremony. The bride and groom also took English names. She became Mary. Kittamaquund became King Charles. He liked the idea of having the same name as the king of England. Indeed, he liked many things about the colonists. King Charles stopped painting his face and particularly liked to wear English clothes. He even sent his seven-year-old daughter, Princess Mary, to live with Margaret and Mary Brent, so that she could learn the English ways.

Not Just Plain Leonard

*B*y 1642, Maryland was growing nicely, even though St. Mary's wasn't the city that Cecil had hoped for. There were a few more large houses, but too many colonists wanted to grow tobacco. They discovered it was more profitable than fur trading or anything else they could do. Tobacco was so important, in fact, that it was used instead of money. Each new batch of settlers moved farther and farther away from St. Mary's in search of land for their tobacco plantations. They were now too busy and too far away to attend meetings of the General Assembly. Instead, they elected others to represent them.

That year, the planters were so pleased with the way things were going and the way Leonard was running the colony that the assembly voted to thank Lord Baltimore for his "great charge and solicitude in maintaining the government and protecting

the inhabitants in their persons, rights, and liberties." Besides their thanks, the assembly ordered that every resident of Maryland over the age of twelve contribute fifteen pounds of tobacco to help the proprietor with the expenses of running the colony.

Leonard knew from the news that came in with every ship from England that Cecil had more to worry about than his expenses. He had even more enemies than before, which certainly meant more trouble for his colony. And more trouble for Maryland meant more trouble for Leonard. He decided it was time to go to England to talk to Cecil in person. After all, he'd been away for nearly ten years. If there was going to be trouble he wanted to know how his brother felt without waiting six months for Cecil's answer to a letter.

Leonard made Giles Brent lieutenant general, chancellor, admiral, chief magistrate, and commander and put him in charge of the colony. He then set sail for England. When he arrived, Leonard found things were worse than he thought. The Royalist forces of the Anglican King Charles I were actually at war with the forces of the Puritan-controlled Parliament. Cecil was working very hard not to take sides. Leonard could only watch and worry. This was definitely a time to let Cecil do the talking.

Meanwhile, trouble was brewing back in Maryland. Leonard was gone only a few months when a London sea captain named Richard Ingle sailed into the Chesapeake Bay to trade in Virginia and Maryland. Stopping off at Accomac on Virginia's Eastern Shore, he made no secret that he was a Puritan.

"And," he declared loudly to any who cared to listen, "I am a captain for Parliament against the king!"

Some Virginians were listening and reported him to the sheriff, who hurried down to the waterfront to arrest him for treason. When he arrived, the sheriff quickly changed his mind. On the deck of his pinnace, the *Reformation*, Captain Ingle stood with his sword drawn and roared at everyone who came near the ship, "He that come aboard, I cut off his head!" The sheriff believed him, and without a word, turned around and left.

Without a look back, the captain shouted orders to his crew to weigh anchor and sail up the Bay to Maryland. Captain Ingle figured he'd settled the matter of his treasonous words, but in Maryland, Giles Brent, who took the business of being governor very seriously, had other ideas. He had just received an order from King Charles to seize anyone on the side of Parliament. No sooner had the *Reformation* entered Maryland waters than Giles had Richard Ingle arrested for high treason and his ship seized.

Although St. Mary's had a sheriff, the town had no jail. Before long, Puritan sympathizers helped Richard Ingle escape to his ship. As he sailed down the St. Mary's River, he promised himself that he'd be back to rid Maryland of the "wicked Papists," as Catholics were called by their enemies, and to free the colony's Protestants from the "tyrannical government" of the Calverts.

Two Vengeful Men

By the autumn of 1644, when Leonard decided it was time to get back to St. Mary's, England was controlled by the Puritans in Parliament. At any moment, the Parliament could take the Maryland Charter away from Cecil. That was bad enough, but what Cecil and Leonard didn't know was that their time of troubles was just beginning, and not in England, but in Maryland.

Richard Ingle and William Claiborne had waited until just such a time for their revenge on the Calverts and their supporters in Maryland. King Charles could not help them now. William Claiborne had friends on Kent Island eager to take control away from Giles Brent. Throughout Maryland, Protestants resented the Catholic noblemen who had most of the money and power in the colony. All they needed was a leader.

Leonard sensed a change in the feeling of many Marylanders after his return in the autumn of 1644. There was very little sympathy for the king. He learned quickly who his true friends were. The Brents, Thomas Greene, Father White, John Lewger, Robert Vaughn, and a few others stood by Leonard as the leaves on the trees turned red and gold and the wind blew colder and colder.

In February 1645, that same cold wind filled the sails of Richard Ingle's *Reformation*, carrying it up the Bay and into the Potomac River. The ship now was a privateer sailing with the English lord high admiral's permission to capture any ship or person opposed to Parliament. It carried cannon and fighting men who Captain Ingle picked up in Virginia. He chose the most desperate men he could find to go with him to Maryland to plunder the land and homes of the Calverts and their Catholic friends. Their reward for going with him was anything they found and could carry away.

Boldly, Richard Ingle sailed up the St. Mary's River. In his path lay the *Speagle*, a Dutch merchant ship trading in Maryland. It was Ingle's lucky day, but a very unlucky day for Giles Brent, who happened to be aboard the Dutch ship. Captain Ingle seized the *Speagle* and took Giles his prisoner. Puffed up with his success, the privateer captain sailed on to St. Mary's.

Luckily, people ashore saw what happened and sent word to Leonard. He ordered Captain Henry Fleete to call up the St. Mary's militia. Men came running to line up in front of Leonard's house, but when they were assembled in front of him, the captain shook his head. He and Thomas Cornwallis had trained them well, but there just were not enough of them to defend St. Mary's against Ingle's shipload of cutthroats. He and Leonard knew that no more volunteers were coming from the surrounding plantations. Too many of the colonists were on the side of Parliament. They might not approve of a man like Ingle, but they did not openly oppose him. Not for the king and the Calverts.

"You must go to Virginia," Captain Fleete told Leonard. "It will be worse for Maryland if you are taken."

Unhappily, Leonard agreed. He did not like to run away, but he feared the bloodshed if he stayed. Ingle would not kill him, he knew, but the militiamen and any others who opposed Ingle would surely suffer injury or death. Sadly, he ordered his important papers and a few belongings to be packed for a journey. Because Peter Draper died while Leonard was in England, his new secretary, Richard Willan, directed the packing.

With Henry Fleete as their guide, Leonard and a handful of his servants and others, who were still loyal to the king and Lord Baltimore, crossed the St. Mary's River and slipped into the forest to make their way to the Potomac and Virginia. There, they remained in exile for nearly two years.

For those who stayed behind in Maryland, those two years were called "the plundering time." Everyone had horrible stories to tell.

Father White, John Lewger, and Giles Brent were all sent back to England as prisoners.

Richard Ingle and his followers, along with friends of William Claiborne, went through the colony taking whatever they wanted, especially from Catholics and those who supported the Calverts and the king. When her brother was arrested, Margaret Brent was at Giles's house on Kent Island. The rebels, as they were called, overran the Brents' plantation. Margaret was forced to flee to St. Mary's where she hid with friends. Which was just as well. She did not have to see their barn set ablaze and their supply of corn burned. She did not have to watch as their servants were taken prisoner, their cattle killed, and their silver, jewelry, and other valuables carried off.

Thomas Cornwallis was in England when Ingle and his Puritan force raided Maryland. They plundered his plantation and his brand-new house. They took his tobacco, killed his cattle, hogs, and goats or chased them into the woods, took his servants prisoners, ripped up the floors of the house, and stole everything of value, even the locks from the doors and glass from the windows.

With the holds of the *Reformation* and the captured Dutch ship full of plundered goods, Richard Ingle returned to England in May 1645. That did not end the plundering time though. He left a group of Protestants loyal to Parliament in charge of Maryland's government.

In a letter written later to Cecil, those who lived through this time of troubles told him, "Great and many have been the miseries, calamities, and other sufferings which your poor distressed people have sustained here since the beginning of this heinous rebellion put in practice by the pirate Ingle." For two years, they wrote, "most of your Lordship's loyal friends were spoiled of their whole estate and sent away as banished persons out of the province."

Maryland was in a sorry state. Five or six hundred people lived in the colony when Ingle seized St. Mary's. By some counts, only one hundred were left at the beginning of 1646. Many of the largest houses and plantations, which belonged mainly to

Catholics, lay in ruins. Food was scarce. It was a cold, hard winter. As the survivors wrote, "Those few that remained were plundered and deprived of all livelihood and subsistence under that intolerable yoke they were forced to bear under those rebels," who took the "government of your Lordship's province unto themselves...."

The center of that government was Leonard's house. It was taken over by Nathaniel Pope, a Protestant merchant on the side of Parliament and the Puritans. It was called Pope's Fort, because around it was built a tall palisade, guarded by a cannon or two for good measure.

Maryland Reclaimed

Leonard was not sitting idly in Virginia while the rebels were in control of Maryland. With the help of Sir William Berkeley, Virginia's governor, he raised a small army of anti-Puritan Virginians and Marylanders who had fled during the plundering time. Leonard promised to pay the soldiers when they got to Maryland, and he regained control of the colony. By the summer of 1646, Leonard was ready. He loaded soldiers, guns, and supplies onto several small ships and sailed up the Potomac and into the St. Mary's River.

Along the way, Leonard put some of his soldiers ashore to let everyone know that he was back, and Maryland was again under

Lord Baltimore's rule. The army had a very easy time of it. What rebels they found were not feeling very rebellious anymore.

At St. Mary's, Leonard was greeted by Margaret Brent and Thomas Greene. With them was John Lewger. He and Giles spent only a short time as prisoners when they got to England, and as soon as they were free again, they joined Thomas Cornwallis in suing Richard Ingle for the many problems he caused and all the damage he did to their property. All three eventually returned to Maryland. Father White did not fare as well. As an official of the Roman Catholic Church, he was treated harshly by England's Puritan government. He went to prison and then was exiled from England to Belgium. His fate was never to return to the colony he helped to found and loved probably more than anyone else.

Soon after his return, Leonard was dealing with old problems. Kent Island, as usual, was at the top of his list. The independent islanders still did not want Lord Baltimore telling them what to do. Finally, Leonard sent Captain Robert Vaughn and a group of militia men to bring law and order to the island. The militia quickly captured most of the troublemakers and chased the rest to Virginia. In April 1647, Leonard himself went to Kent Island to offer the captured rebels a pardon if they took an oath of allegiance to Lord Baltimore. Most of them did, and before he left, Leonard appointed local officials from among the islanders. With any luck, that would stop some of their complaining.

Sailing down the Bay afterward, Leonard was well pleased with his visit. In fact, he was feeling better about everything than he had since he made his trip to England. His mind was already busy with plans for all the things he had to do. For the first time in a long time, Maryland was at peace and he could get back to work on making the colony grow and prosper.

May found Leonard busy from dawn to dusk. Once more his servants were working in the fields and gardens. They would have a good harvest come fall. Most of the houses and other buildings in St. Mary's and throughout the province were repaired and new ones were going up. Leonard had some of the first horses in Maryland. He rode out in the mornings to look over the corn and tobacco fields, check on new buildings, and make plans.

Then, one morning in early June, he didn't feel like going for his usual ride. By nightfall, he went early to bed with a fever. The next morning, a very worried Richard Willan sent for the doctor. Nothing the doctor did seemed to do any good. King Charles, tayak of the Piscataway, sent his medicine man with his special potions of roots and herbs, but Leonard only grew weaker. Father Francis Ankatill arrived and began to pray. Thomas Greene and Margaret Brent came to be with him, and people gathered outside the palisade. They waited silently.

Leonard knew he was dying. He was sorry to go and leave so many things undone. Thomas Greene sat by his bed and wrote down his wishes. To his godson, Leonard Greene, he left a fine mare. To Richard Willan, he left his cloth suit. He had little else in the way of personal things to give away, just thirteen books, the bed on which he lay, a kneeling desk, a cross made of bone, a gold box of holy relics, several boxes and trunks, a table and chairs, pewter dishes and spoons, three guns, six horses, and a saddle and bridle.

As for his houses and lands and the many things that were his responsibility as the governor of Maryland and the brother of

Lord Baltimore, Leonard beckoned for Thomas Greene and Margaret Brent to come close to his bed.

"You will be the governor," he told Thomas.

He then turned to Margaret, "I make you my sole executrix," he said. "Take all and pay all." And soon after that, on June 11, 1647, Leonard Calvert died. He was forty-one. He would have been pleased to know what Father White wrote of him when the news of his death reached England.

In the opinion of Father White and others who knew him, he may have been only Sir George Calvert's second son, but he was not just plain Leonard. He was Maryland's first governor and, as Father White wrote, he "led the colonists and by wise and humane measures won the friendship of the Indians, the confidence of his sovereign, the Proprietor, and his fellow colonists, and brought the plan to successful fruition."

An Afterword

Leonard Calvert could not have left his affairs, or those of the colony, in any better hands than those of Margaret Brent. Shortly after the governor's death, the soldiers who came with Leonard from Virginia to win back the colony after Ingle's rebellion demanded the pay they were promised. Leonard left very little money and the rest of his and Lord Baltimore's wealth in Maryland was in houses, land, and livestock. When the soldiers learned of Leonard's death, they marched into St. Mary's and demanded their pay.

The government had no money, so Thomas Greene and the council turned to Margaret Brent. They gave her the authority to act as Lord Baltimore's attorney. First, she took all of Leonard's houses and land and Cecil's cattle and sold them to raise enough money to pay the soldiers and avert a crisis. Lord Baltimore had no idea of the actual conditions in his colony and was angry that Margaret Brent sold his cattle. The General Assembly came to her defense. "We do verily believe that it was better for the colony's safety at that time in her hands than in any man's else in the whole province after your brother's death, for the soldiers would never have treated any other with that civility and respect, and though they were ever ready at times to mutiny, yet she still pacified them."

Historical Notes

Page 8 - King James I (1566–1625)

Page 9 - Catholics could not worship in public and they could not hold public office. They had to pay extra taxes, and if they held Catholic services in public they were punished. Those who were suspected of being Catholics were tested by demanding that they swear allegiance to the king as ruler of England and as the head of the Church of England, also called the Anglican Church. Catholics could not swear allegiance to the leader of another church. They believed they owed allegiance only to the head of the Roman Catholic Church, the Pope. They were fined if they did not attend services of the Church of England. By not practicing his religion, George Calvert was able to hold high government office. When Sir George decided it was time to tell the king that he was a Roman Catholic, he had to give up his job as secretary of state.

Page 10 - Leonard's mother, Ann Mynne, died in August 1621. George Calvert apparently married Joan, about whom little is known, some time between 1621 and the birth of their son Philip Calvert in 1626.

Page 16 – We do not know much about Leonard's brother and sisters, Francis, Elizabeth, or Dorothy either. They do not appear in later records, and it is likely that they were lost with Lady Joan.

Page 14 – King Charles I (1600–1649, beheaded).

Page 27 – The half of the ship's mainsail that fell into the sea was retrieved and mended.

Page 29 – Other conditions that may have contributed to their deaths were dehydration from lack of drinking water, the sudden change from cold to hot weather, and unsanitary living conditions.

Page 33 – The first English colonists arrived at Jamestown, Virginia, in 1607. The Indians tried to drive the Englishmen away. Although they killed many of the early Virginians, the Indians could not stop the settlers from taking the land where they had always hunted and grown corn and other vegetables. Many Indians died, too, killed by the colonists' guns, by starvation, and by diseases the English brought to the New World. In the early days of the Virginia colony, Pocahontas and other friendly Indians brought food that kept the settlers at Jamestown alive during their first hard winter.

Page 52 – The colonists were made ill by new strains of diseases unknown in England, to which they had not built up an immunity.

Page 59 – We do not know what actually went on at this first General Assembly. We only know of Cecil's response.

Page 61 – William Claiborne was an agent for Clobery & Company.

Page 78 – Father White did return to England and lived there under the protection of the Calverts until his death in 1656.

Page 81 – If Giles Brent had not been in England, Leonard probably would have made him his executor instead of Margaret.

Glossary

allegiance - loyalty to a government, a king, or other ruler.

Anglican Church - the Church of England, which later became the Episcopal Church in the United States.

banish - to send a person away, usually out of a country.

baron - a nobleman; in Great Britain, also a member of the House of Lords.

barony - the land governed by a baron.

barracks - a building for housing soldiers.

chancellor - the chief government administrator or the secretary to a king or nobleman.

charter - a document giving a person or company permission to establish a colony and telling how it was to be governed.

chief justice - the judge in charge of a court.

Church of England - established in the early 1500s, when King Henry VIII broke all ties with the Catholic Church in Rome and declared himself head of the English church instead of the Pope.

commissioners - people chosen to be in charge of particular jobs; in this story, those chosen by Cecil Calvert to establish his colony in Maryland.

cooper - a barrel maker.

corn pone - a simple form of corn bread.

crow's nest - a platform for a lookout near the top of a ship's mast.

cutthroat - any murderous or dangerous person; originally a person who cut people's throats.

defame - to attack a person's reputation with false information.

dominion - an area ruled by one person or group.

dunce - a stupid or ignorant person.

earthenware - pottery or ceramics, often glazed and decorated, in which food was served and eaten.

executrix - a woman assigned to carry out the orders in a person's will. A man would be called an executor.

exile - when a person is driven out of his or her native country or home.

freeman - a person who is a free citizen, not a slave, with voting and other rights.

fruition - achievement of a desired result.

gangplank - a movable bridge used by people to board or leave a boat at a wharf or pier.

governess - a woman who is a private teacher in charge of educating children.

grazier - a person who raises sheep or cattle for market; he grazes them to fatten them up.

heinous - hateful.

knight - in England, a title given to a person by the king, especially for his service or personal worth.

magistrate - a government official who sees that laws are carried out.

master (of a ship) - another word for captain of a ship.

militia - a group of men called for military service in times of emergency.

musket - a heavy, long-barreled gun.

musketeer - a soldier armed with a musket.

mutiny - a rebellion against people in authority; in this story, soldiers against the colonial government.

pacified - made peaceful, calm.

palisade - a fence of pointed stakes, or pales, used for defense.

papist - a degrading or belittling word for Roman Catholic.

Parliament - the legislature of Great Britain.

persecute - to harrass or punish, often for belief or religion.

pinnace - a light sailing ship.

plantation - originally, a colony or settlement; later, large individual pieces of land, usually used for farming, especially tobacco in early Maryland.

plunder - to openly rob people of their valuables and other belongings.

potion - a drink supposed to have medicinal, poisonous, or magical powers.

powder and shot - the gunpowder and lead ball used as ammunition in a musket.

privateer - a privately armed warship with government permission to fight and capture enemy ships; a person on such a vessel.

proprietor - an owner.

province - another word for colony.

Puritans - English Protestants who didn't like the Church of England's elaborate ceremonies. They wanted to purify the Church of England and live strictly by the Bible.

relics - the remains of something from the past; here, something belonging to a saint or other sacred person.

Royalist - a supporter of the king.

run aground - when a boat or ship hits the bottom beneath the water, or runs up on shore.

salt meat - beef, pork, or fish cured or preserved with salt for later use. Usually stored in barrels.

sawyer - a person who cuts wood with a saw.

sloop - a single-masted sailing vessel; a type of boat once very popular for sailing on the Chesapeake Bay.

sovereign - a king or other ruler.

steward - a person who manages another's household, financial, or other affairs.

tayak - the emperor of an Indian tribe.

toast - to have a drink in honor of a person, thing, or event.

Tower of London - the fortress that was once a palace and later a prison.

to wit - that is to say; namely.

treason - disloyalty in words or acts to a sovereign or country to which a person owes allegiance.

trifle - something of very little value.

tutor - a private teacher.

tyrannical - unjustly harsh or cruel; a tyrant is an unjust or oppressive ruler.

verily - really; in truth.

wattle and daub - a method of building with stakes or tree branches, or wattles, plastered with mud or clay, called daub.

werowance - the chief of an Indian village.

Index

Calvert *(cont.)*
George, Jr., 10, 13, 19, 21, 25,
27, 30, 53, 66; George, Sr.,
8–16, 18, 32, 45, 81, 86; Grace,
11; Helen, 10, 13; Lady Joan,
10, 14, 15, 32, 86; Philip, 86
canoe, 36; log canoe, 37
Catholic(s), 8, 9, 15, 21, 22, 30, 42,
56, 72–75, 77, 78, 85, 86
chancellor, 71
Charles I (King of England), 14,
15, 16, 32, 71, 72, 73, 86
Charles (Kittamaquund), 68, 79
charter. *See* Maryland Charter
Chesapeake Bay, 15, 32, 33, 35,
36, 59, 62, 71, 79
Chief Justice, 18, 43
Chief Magistrate, 18, 42, 71
Christmas, 29
Church of England, 9, 14, 15, 85
Claiborne, William, 15, 32–36, 59,
60–62, 67, 73, 75, 87
clapboard, 56
Clobery & Company, 87
Cockatrice, 60
commissioners, 18, 22, 30, 57
cooper, 56
Cornwallis, Thomas, 18, 21, 22,
43, 48, 56–58, 60, 62, 64, 65,
74, 76, 78
Cowes, 22, 23, 37

Cox, Ann, 29

diseases, 52, 53, 87
Dove, 20, 23, 25, 26, 29, 31, 39, 41
Draper, Peter, 19, 20, 21, 46, 47,
48, 75
Duke of Buckingham, 12
Dutch, 74, 76

Easter, 52
Eastern Shore (Virginia), 72
Edwards, Richard, 29, 53
emperor. *See* tayak
England, 7, 9–16, 18, 22, 23, 25,
28, 33, 35, 37, 41, 43, 45, 50,
51, 53, 56, 57, 59, 61, 66, 67,
68, 71, 73, 75, 76, 78, 81, 85,
87
English Channel, 22
Evelyn, George, 61–65

Fleet, Henry, 39– 41, 43, 44, 46,
60, 74, 75
Florida, 17
food, 14, 20, 26, 29, 30–33, 44, 48,
50, 51, 57, 77
fort, 22, 41, 48, 49
freemen, 57–59, 65, 66
French, 11–13
fur trading, 15, 33, 34, 39, 59, 61,
69